THE PIANO

Where does music come from? Is it something that you learn? Or is it simply given to you – and nobody knows where it comes from?

The young boy in this story is not good at school. He is not good at learning words or numbers. He likes to sing with the other boys and girls; but he is not good at singing. He does not get the first job that he tries to get. He is a nice boy, but he is not good at anything special.

And then he finds a piano. He also finds that he can play the piano. So, perhaps we can say that he does not find music, but that music finds him.

OXFORD BOOKWORMS LIBRARY
Human Interest

The Piano ·

Stage 2 (700 headwords)

Series Editor: Jennifer Bassett
Founder Editor: Tricia Hedge
Activities Editors: Jennifer Bassett and Alison Baxter

ROSEMARY BORDER

The Piano

OXFORD UNIVERSITY PRESS

OXFORD
UNIVERSITY PRESS

Great Clarendon Street, Oxford OX2 6DP

Oxford University Press is a department of the University of Oxford.
It furthers the University's objective of excellence in research, scholarship,
and education by publishing worldwide in

Oxford New York

Auckland Cape Town Dar es Salaam Hong Kong Karachi
Kuala Lumpur Madrid Melbourne Mexico City Nairobi
New Delhi Shanghai Taipei Toronto

With offices in

Argentina Austria Brazil Chile Czech Republic France Greece
Guatemala Hungary Italy Japan Poland Portugal Singapore
South Korea Switzerland Thailand Turkey Ukraine Vietnam

OXFORD and OXFORD ENGLISH are registered trade marks of
Oxford University Press in the UK and in certain other countries

© Oxford University Press 2000

The moral rights of the author have been asserted

Database right Oxford University Press (maker)

First published in Oxford Bookworms 1989

14 16 18 19 17 15

No unauthorized photocopying

ISBN-13: 978 0 19 422982 1
ISBN-10: 0 19 422982 3

A complete recording of this Bookworms edition of
The Piano is available on cassette ISBN 0 19 422886 x

Printed in Hong Kong

Illustrated by: Julie Joubinaux

CONTENTS

Chapter 1

In the Dressing-room

SIR ANTHONY EVANS PLAYS LISZT. The words above the door of the theatre were a metre high. On the wall there was a big picture of Sir Anthony at the piano. Hundreds of people were waiting outside the ticket office. It was Sir Anthony's eightieth birthday concert and everybody wanted a ticket. I had a special ticket, because I was a newspaper reporter. I wanted to talk to the famous pianist before his concert. I showed my ticket to the doorman and went into the theatre. Then I walked upstairs to the dressing-rooms.

On my way upstairs I thought about the famous pianist. I was a little afraid. My mouth was dry and my hands were shaking.

I arrived outside the dressing-room.

There was a big gold star on the door.

I knocked, and a tall man opened it. He was very old, but his eyes were blue and bright. He was wearing black trousers and a beautiful white shirt. He had a lot of straight, silvery hair. He looked just like his picture on the wall of the theatre.

'My name's Sally Hill,' I began. 'I . . .'

1

Hundreds of people were waiting outside the ticket office.

The old man saw my notebook and smiled at me.

'Don't tell me. You're a reporter. Which newspaper do you work for?'

'*The Sunday Times,* sir.'

'A very good newspaper. Come in and sit down. Ask your questions. We were young once, weren't we, Linda? But of course that was a long time ago.'

He turned to a tall woman, who was standing in the corner. She smiled at me with friendly brown eyes. 'So this is Lady Evans,' I thought. 'What a nice face she has! She looks like a farmer's wife.'

I was not afraid any more. I sat down and opened my notebook.

'Tell me about yourself, please, Sir Anthony. Did you come from a musical family? Did you start to learn the piano when you were three, like Mozart?'

The famous pianist smiled. 'No, no, my dear. I am the first musician in my family. And I was fourteen years old before I touched a piano for the first time.' He saw the surprise on my face. 'We have a little time before my concert. I'll tell you my story. It's a strange story, but every word of it is true. You see, I left school when I was thirteen. Everybody called me Tony in those days. I worked on a farm . . .'

It was an exciting story and he told it well. At first I

tried to write everything down in my notebook. Then the pen fell from my hand and I just listened. I was lost in Sir Anthony's wonderful story. He told me about an old school behind a high wall in a dirty street. There was broken glass on top of the wall. The school yard was very small. As he spoke, pictures came into my mind. I saw a little boy called Tony Evans, playing football with an old tin . . .

Chapter 2

A Poor Boy

The teacher's name was Mr Grey. He was grey, like his name: he was old and grey and tired. Everything about him was grey: grey suit, grey shirt, grey hair and a long, thin, grey face. When he smiled the children saw his long, grey teeth. But he did not often smile. Mr Grey did not enjoy his job. He did not like children.

'Why does he work here?' one of the children asked one day. 'He doesn't like us.'

'But he likes the long school holidays!' said Tony. The other children laughed. They thought that was a very clever answer.

But Tony was not a clever boy. He was big and slow and silent. He did not enjoy his lessons. Usually he just sat at his desk and waited quietly for four o'clock to come, when he could go home.

But Tuesday mornings were different, because Tuesday was music day. Every Tuesday morning an old lady called Mrs Lark came to the school. Mrs Lark played the piano and the children sang. She was not a very good pianist, but she liked children and she enjoyed her work. She knew a lot of songs too. Every Tuesday her fat little fingers flew like birds up and down the keys of the piano. The children sang like birds, too. Then twelve o'clock came. Mrs Lark said 'goodbye' and locked up the piano for another week.

The children sang like birds.

The musician shook his head and pushed his little piano away.

Tony did not often hear music. His family was poor, and poor people did not often hear music. There was no TV or radio in those days. There were concerts in the town, of course, but poor people did not go to concerts. Sometimes an Italian street musician came to town. He had a little piano on wheels, and a poor thin monkey which sat on top of it. The people came out of their houses to listen to his music. Then the monkey went round with a little tin cup. 'Give us a penny!' sang the musician. But when the monkey came back, the tin cup was always empty. The musician shook his head and pushed his little piano away.

There were six children in the Evans family, and

Tony was the oldest. They lived in a very small house at the end of a long, grey street. The toilet was outside, in the yard. There was no bathroom. Everybody washed in the kitchen. On Saturday evenings everybody in the family had a bath one after another in an old tin bath in front of the fire. It took all evening. Every Monday Mrs Evans washed all the family's clothes in the tin bath. But the Evans were clean and they had enough to eat. Tony did not feel poor, because all his friends were poor too.

In those days, poor children usually left school when they were thirteen. Most of Tony's friends found jobs in shops or factories in the town. Tony did not want to work in a shop or a factory. But he needed a job because his family needed the money.

A few days after his thirteenth birthday, Tony left school too. He began to look for a job. But he was unlucky. The factory did not want him. The shops did not want him. Then his mother thought, 'What about farming?'

One hot summer afternoon she decided to take her son to a farm outside the town.

'I worked on Mr Wood's farm when I was young,' she told Tony. 'Then I met your father and we moved to the town. But I enjoyed farm work, and I think you'll like it too . . . I wrote to Mr Wood last week and asked him to give you a job on the farm. That will be better than the factory.'

Chapter 3

A Farmer's Boy

Tony and his mother got on a bus in the middle of the town. At first they drove through streets of small, grey houses. Then the bus left the town and drove along a country road.

The bus stopped in every village. Tony saw green fields and small, quiet villages. Every house had a garden. The smell of the flowers came in through the open windows of the bus.

At last the bus stopped. Tony could see a river and an old bridge. A small road ran across the bridge, through the fields and over a hill. 'Come on, Tony,' said his mother. They got out of the bus and walked two kilometres in the hot sun. There were white and yellow flowers at the side of the road. Tony did not know their names. He wanted to know more about them. He wanted to know more about the trees too. There were no flowers or trees in his street.

He looked at the cows in the fields.

'I've never seen a real cow,' he said to himself. He

The cows moved slowly through the long green grass.

watched them moving very slowly through the long, green grass. They looked big and quiet.

Tony and his mother arrived at the farmhouse and walked through the farmyard. Chickens were looking for food. A fat white cat sat on a wall and watched them with sleepy eyes.

Mr Wood came to the door and spoke to Tony's mother. 'Hullo, Betty. It's nice to see you again. Thank you for your letter. How are you?' They talked together like old friends.

Tony stood at the door. He felt lost and uncomfortable. But the farmer smiled at him.

'Is this your son, Betty?' he asked.

'Yes. This is Anthony – but we call him Tony at home. He left school two weeks ago. He's a good boy, and he's very strong. Please give him a job, Mr Wood. We need the money. We've got six children, you know.'

The farmer looked at Tony. 'How old are you, boy?' he asked.

'Thirteen, sir.'

'Do you like the country?'

'Yes, sir,' said Tony.

'Would you like to work for me, Tony?' asked Mr Wood. 'Would you like to be a farm boy?'

Tony thought about the factory and the shops. The shops were bad, but the factory was worse. When people came out of the factory in the evening their faces looked white and ill. 'Nothing can be worse than that,' he thought. He looked into the farmer's smiling red face. 'Yes, sir,' he said. 'Yes, please.'

His mother was right. Tony was a good, strong boy and he worked very hard for Mr Wood. The old farmer did not pay him much money. Tony ate his meals in the kitchen and he slept in a little room at the top of the farmhouse. But the farmer was kind to him and taught him a lot. Mr Wood had no sons. He had one daughter. Her name was Linda, and she was a year younger than Tony. Mr Wood loved Linda dearly, but he wanted a son very much. He was like a father to Tony.

Tony was happy. At the end of every day his back was tired and his legs hurt, but he slept like a baby. He ate Mrs Wood's good country food. He drank a lot of milk. Soon he needed new clothes. He sent his old clothes home for his brothers. He sent his family money, too.

Sometimes Tony visited his family. He enjoyed those visits, but he was always happy to leave again. 'I'm a country boy now,' he thought.

He ate Mrs Wood's good country food.

11

In the school holidays Pip and his brother John came to the farm. Pip was seventeen and John was sixteen, but they were both still at school. Their father had a large shoe shop in the town. He wanted them to go to college and learn to be businessmen. But the boys spent all their holidays on Mr Wood's farm.

'I want to be a farmer,' said Pip.

'That's right,' said John. 'Farming is the best job in the world!'

'But you just come here in the summer!' said Tony. 'It isn't always summer, you know. The sun doesn't always shine. Farmers work hard in the winter too. It's a hard, dirty job.'

'But *you* like it!' said John, and he was right. Tony liked his job very much.

Chapter 4

An Old Piano

One hot summer afternoon Tony, John and Pip were cutting the long grass. The sun was hot and they were tired. Mr Wood came into the field.

'Now, boys,' he said, 'I have a job for you.'

'He always has a job for us!' said Pip very quietly. The other boys smiled. The farmer liked to keep them

'Get the rubbish out of the building.'

busy. They walked with him to an old wooden building near the farmhouse.

'Now,' said Mr Wood. 'My new car will arrive here next week. I want this building for a garage. Get the rubbish out of the building. Then clean it really well. I want to keep the car in it.'

'What shall we do with the rubbish, Mr Wood?' asked Pip.

'Get rid of it, of course!' answered the farmer. 'Now stop asking questions, young Pip. I'm a busy man.' He walked away.

The three boys opened the doors of the building. They looked at the rubbish, then they looked at each other.

'This is going to take a long time,' said Tony.

He went to the back of the building. He saw something behind a lot of old boxes. It was very big.

'What's this?' asked Tony.

'Is it a cupboard?' asked Pip.

John came and moved some of the boxes. 'It isn't a cupboard,' he said in surprise. 'It's an old piano.'

The piano was made of beautiful, dark brown wood. Tony took off his shirt and cleaned the wood with it. He saw brightly-coloured birds, flowers and leaves. They shone like stars in the dark, dirty building. Tony opened the piano. He looked at the keys.

14

'We can't get rid of this,' he said. 'We really can't.' He found an old, broken chair and sat down at the piano. His fingers touched the keys. He closed his eyes. Half-forgotten music danced through his mind. His fingers began to move. They moved up and down the keys. He began to play an old song. He was suddenly very happy.

'I can play the piano,' he thought. 'Nobody taught me, but my mind tells my fingers what to do, and I can make music.'

His friends listened.

'That's beautiful,' said John. 'What is it?'

'I don't know,' said Tony.

Tony's fingers moved up and down the piano keys.

They heard a noise behind them. Linda Wood was standing at the door. She was a tall, thin girl with long, soft brown hair. She was not beautiful, but she had big, kind brown eyes and a sweet smile. She was smiling now, and she was singing very quietly.

Tony heard her and stopped playing. He stood up. His face was red and he felt hot and uncomfortable.

'Don't stop, Tony,' said Linda.

'I've finished,' said Tony shortly. He closed the piano.

Linda came into the building. 'Look,' she said, 'Mother has sent you some cakes and milk. She asked me to bring them.'

'Mother has sent you some cakes and milk.'

Mrs Wood was a very good cook. The cakes were still warm . . . They all ate and drank.

Linda looked at the piano. 'Who taught you to play the piano, Tony?' she asked.

Tony looked down at his dirty old shoes. 'I can't play the piano,' he said.

'Yes, you can!' said Linda. 'I heard you. I have piano lessons at school, but I can't play like you. I like that song. It's called *Green Fields*. I've got the music at school, but I can't play it. It's too difficult for me. Do you want to borrow it?'

'I can't read music,' said Tony. 'We didn't have music lessons at my school.' He looked unhappy and thoughtful. 'Music!' thought Tony. He remembered the street musician with his little monkey. Then he thought about Mrs Lark. He remembered those wonderful Tuesday mornings, and he smiled. 'We sang a little on Tuesday mornings, that's all,' he said.

He stood and looked at the piano. 'I must have it,' he said to himself. 'I'll ask Mr Wood.'

At seven o'clock Tony washed in cold water and put on his clean shirt. Then he went to the kitchen with Pip and John. They sat down at the big kitchen table and Mrs Wood put the food on three hot plates. Then she went to have supper with Mr Wood and Linda.

Tony ate his meat and potatoes and drank two cups

of strong, sweet tea. Then he had three small cakes and an apple. He was always hungry. He washed his plate and his cup and put them away.

'Now!' he thought. He got up and went to the door.

'Where are you going?' asked John.

'I want to ask Mr Wood about that piano,' said Tony. 'Pianos cost a lot of money. We must tell him about this one. Then he can decide what to do with it.' He knocked at the door of the sitting-room.

'Come in!' said the farmer. He was reading his *Farmer's Weekly*. Mrs Wood was mending a hole in Linda's school dress. Linda herself was doing her homework at the table in the corner.

'Please, Mr Wood,' began Tony, 'there's an old piano in that building . . .'

'I don't want to know, boy!' said Mr Wood.

'You don't want to know?' said Tony. 'But a piano isn't rubbish, sir . . .'

'It *is* rubbish, boy. Take it away. Get rid of it. I want that building for my new car. Now go away. I'm tired. I've had a busy day and I want to read my newspaper.'

'But . . .' began Tony again.

'I don't want to know!' said Mr Wood. 'Go away!' He shook his newspaper angrily.

'Yes, Mr Wood,' said Tony. He went out and closed the door behind him. He came back into the kitchen.

'Mr Wood, there's an old piano in that building.'

'Listen – can you help me?' he said to Pip and John. 'Mr Wood doesn't want that old piano. He says I can have it. He wants the building for his new car. I can have the piano if I want it. And oh, yes – I want it very much. But where can I put it?'

'That's easy,' said Pip. 'We can put it on Mr Wood's lorry. We can take the piano to your house. Your family will love it!'

'You've never seen our house,' said Tony. 'It's very small, and there are seven people living in it. We can't take the piano there.'

'Sell it, then,' said John. 'Buy something nice with the money.'

'I don't want money,' said Tony. 'I want the piano.'

'How can I tell them?' he thought. 'How can I tell them how I feel about it?' He looked at his hands. He wanted to feel the black and white keys under his fingers again. He wanted to hear the music in his mind . . . 'What's happening to me?' he thought.

Pip looked at the clock. 'It's late,' he said. 'And I'm tired. I'm going to go to bed. We can think about your piano tomorrow.'

Chapter 5

The Village School

The next morning the boys got up at six o'clock. They took some sandwiches and a bottle of cold tea, and they began to cut the long grass in Mr Wood's biggest field.

The field was near a quiet road. At the side of the road was a small school. It stood in a garden. There were flowers and vegetables and a few fruit trees. But no children were there. The school was empty. It was summer and the children were on holiday.

The sun shone down angrily. The boys were hot and thirsty. At eleven o'clock Tony went for a drink, but the bottle was empty.

'I want a drink of water,' he said to Pip and John. He took the empty bottle and went into the school garden. There was a tap there and he turned it. No water came out. He went to the door of the school. He pushed – and it opened.

There was a little kitchen. Tony turned on the tap. He took a long drink and filled his bottle. Then he decided to look around the little school. It did not take him long. There was one classroom. The desks and chairs were very small, because it was a school for young children. Tony went back into the kitchen. 'It's July,' he thought. 'Everyone is on holiday. School doesn't start again until September. I can put the piano here. No one will come here. I've got six weeks. And in six weeks perhaps I can find a home for my piano.'

He went back to the field.

'You were away a long time,' said Pip. 'Did you have a drink, or a holiday?' They all laughed.

'Listen,' said Tony. 'The school door is open. The school's empty. I'm going to put my piano in the classroom.'

'Don't be stupid!' said John. 'What will the teacher say?'

'He won't say anything! He's on holiday,' said Tony. 'You're on holiday too, aren't you? When do you go back to school?'

'*I'm going to put my piano in the classroom.*'

'September the ninth,' said John.

'That's right!' said Tony. 'Listen – the door's open. The key's in the door. I'm not going to steal anything. I'm just going to keep the piano in the classroom for a week or two . . . Can you help me? We'll put the piano on the lorry, and we'll take it to the school.'

'When?' asked Pip.

'Tonight,' said Tony.

The three boys worked very hard. They cleaned out the building. They cleaned the windows too. Then they put the piano on Mr Wood's lorry.

'What time are we going?' asked Pip.

'Eight o'clock,' answered Tony.

Linda gave the boys their supper that night. Mrs Wood was at a meeting in the village.

'Boys,' said Linda, 'Father says you are borrowing the lorry tonight.'

'Yes, that's right,' said Pip. 'I'm driving.'

'Please, can you take me to the village? Catherine is ill.' Catherine was Linda's best friend. 'I want to visit her.'

'But . . .' began Tony. He looked into her kind brown eyes and he told her his story. He told her about his old school. He told her about Mrs Lark. He talked about the village school, and the open door, and the quiet, empty classroom. Linda listened. John and Pip listened too. Then Linda smiled.

23

The boys drove the lorry to the little school.

'Thank you, Tony. Now I understand. And I want to help you.'

The boys drove Linda to Catherine's house.

'Please come back at half past nine,' she said to Pip. She spoke loudly because Catherine's mother was listening. Then she said, very quietly, 'Good luck, Tony – and be careful!'

The boys drove the lorry to the little school. Then they moved the piano. It was very heavy, but they were young and strong. They pushed it into the classroom and stood it against a wall.

'It looks beautiful here,' said Pip. He touched the keys. They made a loud, unmusical noise.

'Listen to that!' said his brother. 'You had piano lessons for three years, but you didn't learn anything. Play something for us, Tony.'

Tony sat down and began to play one of Mrs Lark's songs. The music sang in his mind. It travelled along his arms. His fingers danced over the keys. He did not look at his hands. He did not look at the keys. His eyes were closed. He was in another world.

His friends listened. Tony was not clever. He was big and quiet and slow. But there was music in his big, strong hands.

That summer was a happy time for Tony. Every evening after supper he borrowed Linda's bicycle. He cycled to the school, and he played the piano. When it was dark he cycled back to the farm again. He was afraid to turn on a light in the school. He did not want anybody to see him.

'I think Tony has a girlfriend,' said Mrs Wood to Linda. Linda just smiled.

Tony learned to read music. Linda brought him a book of easy songs. She showed him the music. He looked at the little black notes and the five thin black lines on the pages of the book.

'This is easy,' he said to Linda. 'It's like writing. The notes tell your fingers what to do.'

Tony learned to read music.

'That's right,' said Linda. She showed him the long notes and the short notes. She taught him to read the words at the top of the page.

'Look!' she said. 'That's Italian. *Lento* – slow.'

But Tony was not slow. He learned very fast. Linda was a good teacher. Both of them enjoyed her lessons.

Chapter 6

Mr Gordon finds a Musician

Mr Gordon was the teacher at the little village school. He was a kind old man and the children liked him. They enjoyed his lessons and he enjoyed teaching them. There was no piano at the school. This sometimes made him a little unhappy, because he loved music very much. But he sang with the children. He filled their young minds with songs and stories. It was a happy school.

One night during the summer holidays Mr Gordon wanted a book. He looked everywhere.

'I know!' he said suddenly. 'I left it at school. I'll go there at once. It isn't far away.'

He walked through the school garden. The door of the school was open! He felt in his pocket for the key – it was not there!

'Oh dear!' thought Mr Gordon. 'I forgot to lock the door. Now somebody is in the school. Perhaps it's a thief! What can I do?' Then he heard the music . . .

Tony played the same line of music again and again. It was not easy.

'*Prestissimo,*' said the words at the top of the page. 'Very fast.' His fingers flew over the keys.

Mr Gordon stood and listened. There was a happy smile on his face. Then Tony stopped playing.

'That wasn't right,' he said to himself. He looked carefully at the little black notes on their thin black lines. 'The left hand goes like this.'

Mr Gordon spoke. 'And the right hand goes like this . . .'

Tony turned round. His face was white. 'Don't tell the police,' he said. 'Please. I haven't stolen anything. I haven't done anything wrong.'

'No, no, of course not,' said the teacher. 'But who are you? What are you doing in my classroom? And how did this piano get here?'

Mr Gordon visited the farm and talked to Mr and Mrs Wood.

'Tony is very special,' said Mr Gordon. 'I have been a teacher for forty years, but I have never met a boy like Tony. He must have music lessons at once. Then

Mr Gordon stood and listened.

'I came to school for a book, but I found a musician!'

he must go to the College of Music in London. He needs to work with other musical boys and girls.'

'But his mother and father are poor,' said Mrs Wood. 'They can't pay for music lessons. They can't send him to college. They have five small children at home. Tony sends them money every month.'

'I can give Tony his first lessons,' said Mr Gordon. 'I don't want any money – I'll be very happy to teach this wonderful boy. I feel – oh, how can I explain to you? . . . This is a very exciting time for me. Last night I came to school to look for a book, and I found a musician! . . . But Tony learns very quickly. Soon he will need a really good teacher. Then we'll have to think about money. Perhaps Tony can go to the

College of Music in the daytime and work in a restaurant in the evenings . . .'

'No, he can't!' said Mr Wood. Suddenly his face was red and angry.

'Tony is a good boy. He's like a son to us. His father is poor, but we are not.'

'That's right!' said his wife. She was usually a quiet woman, but her eyes were bright and excited. '*We* will send Tony to the College of Music,' she said.

Tony knew nothing about their conversation. He was cleaning Mr Wood's new car when Mr Gordon visited the farm. But that visit changed his life. Mr Wood had a quiet talk with him later.

'Mr Gordon wants to give you piano lessons,' he told Tony.

Tony's eyes shone like stars. Then he shook his head. 'I haven't any money, sir,' he said.

'Mr Gordon doesn't want any money. I've had a talk with him. You are going to go to the school at four o'clock every afternoon. You will have your lesson, and you will practise on the piano for two hours. Then you'll come back to the farm and have your supper.'

'But my work . . .' began Tony.

'I can find another farm boy,' said Mr Wood, 'but good musicians are special people. Give me three tickets for your first concert, and I'll be happy.'

Chapter 7

The Music Competition

Tony worked and worked. He got up at six every morning. He worked on the farm until four o'clock in the afternoon. But every minute of the day, music filled his mind.

At four o'clock he cycled to his piano lesson with Mr Gordon. He practised until seven o'clock, then he cycled back to the farm for supper. After supper he read Mr Gordon's music books. Often he fell asleep at the kitchen table.

At night, while he slept, his mind was still full of music. Small black notes danced in front of his eyes. When he woke up the music was still there. Tony lived in a world of music.

The leaves fell from the trees. Winter came. It was dark when Tony got up in the mornings. It was dark when he cycled to his piano lesson, and it was dark when he cycled back to the farm again. Sometimes it snowed. Then he had to walk to and from the school. But he never missed a lesson.

'How's the boy getting on?' the farmer asked Mr Gordon one day.

'Very well,' said the teacher. 'But he's too quick for me. Soon he'll need a real teacher.'

Spring came, and the trees were green again.

'There's a music competition in the town on June 12th,' said Mr Gordon one evening.

'Can I go and listen?' asked Tony.

'No,' said his teacher. '*I* will go and listen. *You* are going to play in the competition.'

'But I can't do that! I need to practise more. I'm not ready!' said Tony.

'You will be ready,' said his teacher quietly.

Mr Gordon was a kind old man. But he made Tony practise for four hours every day. Another boy helped Mr Wood on the farm while Tony practised for the competition.

'Two weeks to go before the competition,' said Mr Gordon one evening. 'Look, this is the programme.'

The programme was big and beautiful and expensive. Tony looked for his name. He found it. 'Anthony Evans, aged 15. Piano.'

'Nobody calls me Anthony,' he said. 'Why can't they call me Tony?'

'Tony is a boy's name,' said Mr Gordon. 'Anthony is a man's name. Tony Evans was a farm boy. Anthony Evans is a musician. One day, Anthony Evans will be

The programme was big and beautiful and expensive.

famous all over the world. And from today I'm going to call you Anthony.'

On the morning of the competition Mr and Mrs Wood and Anthony went into town in the car. While Mr Wood had a drink with some friends, Mrs Wood took Anthony shopping. She bought him a new brown suit and a new white shirt. Then she took him into a shoe shop – and Pip's father sold her some new shoes for Anthony.

They were beautiful shoes. They shone like glass and Mrs Wood liked them very much. The shoes were too small and they hurt Anthony's feet. But he did not say anything – what could he say?

Mrs Wood paid for the shoes, and Pip's father put them in a box.

'I hear you're playing in the music competition tonight,' he said to Anthony. 'I saw your name in the programme. Anthony Evans – it sounds wonderful. Good luck!'

In the evening the Wood family and Anthony drove to Mr Gordon's house. Mr Gordon came out. He was wearing his best suit.

'You look wonderful, Mr Gordon!' laughed Mrs Wood. 'Are you getting married?'

The old man got into the car and they all drove to the competition. The Woods went to their seats, but Mr Gordon took Anthony through the stage door. He took him to a room behind the stage. A lot of musicians were waiting there. The women were wearing long dresses. The men were wearing evening suits. Nobody spoke to Anthony.

'Goodbye, my boy,' said Mr Gordon, 'and good luck.'

Anthony sat in the waiting room for a long time. His feet hurt. They burned like fire. His hands felt cold. They were shaking. From a long way away he heard the sound of a piano. Every few minutes a man came in and called someone's name. After a long time the man came in and said, 'Mr Evans, please.' Anthony did not move. Nobody usually called him Mr Evans!

'Mr Anthony Evans, please!' said the man again. 'Come along – we haven't got all night!'

Anthony got up. 'Oh, my feet hurt!' he thought. He followed the man up some stairs. 'I'm walking like Charlie Chaplin,' he thought. 'Everybody will laugh at me.'

He walked on to the stage and sat down at the big piano. The dark wood shone like glass. He could see his face in it. He turned round and looked at the sea of faces. He could not see the Wood family. He could not see Mr Gordon. But suddenly Anthony felt their love and their kindness. His feet stopped hurting, his hands stopped shaking. He touched the piano. It was much bigger than the old piano in the classroom. The keys looked very clean and new. He wanted to touch them.

'Well,' he said to himself, 'of course I want to touch them. That's why I'm here!' And he began to play. He forgot about himself. He forgot about all the strange people in the theatre, and he just played for his friends. He played for Mr and Mrs Wood. He played for Linda. He played for Mr Gordon. And he played for old Mrs Lark.

'Where are you now, Mrs Lark?' he thought. 'Do you remember Tony Evans? You gave us a lot of happiness, Mrs Lark. Thank you. Thank you.' His

Beautiful sounds filled the theatre.

hands flew over the piano keys. Beautiful sounds filled the theatre.

'He's going to win the competition,' Mr Gordon said to himself. 'And this is the happiest day of my life.'

And Anthony won the competition. He knew that he was the winner because he saw his photograph in the newspaper the next day. But he could not remember anything about it. All he remembered was his feet.

When he got out of the car, he could not walk. His new shoes hurt him too much. Mr Wood helped him into the kitchen while Mrs Wood filled an old tin bath with warm water. Linda took Anthony's shoes off. His feet were very hot and red. He put them in the warm water.

'This is wonderful,' he said.

'You've won!' shouted Mrs Wood. 'Forget about your feet, boy – you've won the competition! This is the most important night in your life!'

But Anthony was too tired to answer. They helped him up to bed, and he slept until nine o'clock the next morning.

Linda brought him breakfast in bed. He felt very strange and uncomfortable. 'I've never had breakfast in bed before,' he told her.

Chapter 8

The End of the Story

Sir Anthony Evans turned to me. 'That competition was the start of wonderful things for me,' he said. 'I went to the College of Music for three years. Of course, I worked hard, but I enjoyed every minute. I always went back to the farm for my holidays. And one summer, when I was twenty, I asked Miss Linda Wood a very important question. "I can't give you much, Linda," I told her. "But one day I shall be rich and famous. Then I'll come back again, and I'll ask you to marry me." She gave me a long, loving look. Then she laughed. "Oh, Anthony," she said. "Don't wait

until you're rich and famous. Ask me now!" So I did –
and here we are!'

'We've been married for sixty years. Five years ago,
the Queen invited us to Buckingham Palace. I was Mr
Anthony Evans when I went into the Palace. I was Sir
Anthony Evans when I came out . . . and,' – he took his
wife's hand – 'my dear Linda was Lady Evans.'

There was a knock at the door of the dressing-room.
'Two minutes, Sir Anthony!' said a voice.

The famous musician stood up. 'I'm ready,' he said.
He turned to me.

'How many concerts have I given? Two thousand?
Three thousand? For me, every concert is new and
exciting. Now go, my dear, and write your story. Tell
the readers of your newspaper that I am a very lucky
man.'

'We've been married for sixty years.'

GLOSSARY

broken *(adj)* in pieces, or not working

cake something sweet to eat, made of eggs, butter, flour, etc.

classroom a room in a school where children have lessons

clean *(v)* to make something clean (not dirty)

college a school where young people learn to be teachers, doctors, musicians, etc.

competition an event where people sing, play, run, etc. to show who is the best

concert music that people come to listen to, often in a theatre or concert hall

cycle to ride a bicycle

dry not wet

farm *(n)* a place where people grow food and keep animals for food

farmer a person who has a farm

farmhouse the house of a farmer

fall in love with to begin to love somebody very much

fill to make full

grass a plant with thin green leaves that covers fields and gardens

key the black and white pieces of a piano that make music when you touch them

line a long thin mark on paper

lorry a very large 'car' that can carry big things

mind *(n)* the part of you that thinks and feels

monkey an animal with a long tail that lives in trees

note *(n)* a mark on paper that shows a sound in music

piano a large musical instrument

pianist   a person who plays the piano

practise   to do something again and again until you are good at it

programme   a paper that shows what is going to happen, and when

reporter   a person who writes for a newspaper

rid (get rid of)   to take, give or throw something away that you do not want

rubbish   something that you do not want because it is not useful to you

stage   the place inside a theatre where people sing, act, play music, etc.

stage door   the door at the back of a theatre that takes you behind the stage

tap   something that you turn on and water comes out

tin   a kind of metal; a container made of this metal, e.g. a tin of Coke

throw   to move your arm quickly to send something through the air

win *(v)*   to be the best or first person in a competition

yard   a piece of ground next to walls or buildings

The Piano

ACTIVITIES

Before Reading

1 **Read the story introduction on the first page of the book, and the back cover. How much do you know now about the story? Tick one box for each sentence.**

	YES	NO
1 The boy works for a farmer.	☒	☐
2 Everything in the old building is rubbish.	☐	☒
3 The boy has had piano lessons for many years.	☐	☒
4 The boy has never had lessons, but he can play the piano.	☒	☐
5 The boy is clever and does well at school.	☐	☒
6 Music changes the boy's life.	☒	☐

2 **What is going to happen in the story? Can you guess? Tick one box for each sentence.**

	YES	NO
1 The farmer throws the piano away.	☒	☐
2 The farmer gives the piano to the boy.	☐	☒
3 The farmer sells the piano.	☐	☒
4 The boy keeps the piano and learns to play it.	☒	☐
5 The boy loses his job because of the piano.	☒	☐
6 The boy decides to be a music teacher.	☒	☐
7 The story has a happy ending.	☒	☐

While Reading

Read Chapter 1 and answer these questions.

1 How did Sally Hill feel before she met Sir Anthony?
2 Who looked like a farmer's wife?
3 How old was Sir Anthony when he first touched a piano?
4 When did Sir Anthony leave school?
5 Where did he work after he left school?
6 What was Sir Anthony's school like?

Read Chapters 2 and 3. Are these sentences true (T) or false (F)? Change the false sentences into true ones.

1 Mr Grey didn't enjoy teaching children.
2 Tony was a slow, quiet boy.
3 Tuesday was reading day at Tony's school.
4 Tony often went to concerts.
5 There were six children in Tony's family.
6 Most children got jobs in offices when they left school.
7 Tony was interested in the flowers and trees in the country.
8 Mr Wood had a daughter who was older than Tony.
9 On the farm Tony worked hard and slept badly.
10 Pip, John and Tony all liked working on the farm.

Read Chapter 4. Who said these words, and to whom?

1 'It isn't a cupboard. It's an old piano.'
2 'We can't get rid of this. We really can't.'
3 'I have piano lessons at school but I can't play like you.'
4 'It *is* rubbish, boy. Take it away.'
5 'I don't want money. I want the piano.'

Before you read Chapter 5, can you guess the answer to this question?

Tony wants to keep the piano. Will he . . .
1 hide it on the farm?
2 ask Pip and John to keep it in their house?
3 find another place to keep it?
4 ask Mrs Lark to keep it for him?
5 ask Mrs Wood and Linda to help him?

Read Chapter 5. Choose the best question-word for these questions, and then answer them.

Who / Where / Why
1 . . . did Tony go into the school?
2 . . . was the school empty?
3 . . . helped Tony to move the piano?
4 . . . did Tony go every evening that summer?
5 . . . taught Tony to read music?

Read Chapter 6, then circle the correct words in each sentence.

1 Mr Gordon went to the school to get *a key/a book*.
2 Mr Gordon *smiled/cried* when he heard the piano.
3 Tony's first music lessons were *free/cheap*.
4 *Mr Gordon/Mr and Mrs Wood* decided to pay for Tony to go to the College of Music.
5 Mr Wood thought that *good musicians/farm boys* were special people.

Read Chapters 7 and 8. Then put these sentences into the right order, to make a short paragraph.

1 Tony practised for the competition for four hours every day.
2 But he always went back to the farm for his holidays.
3 The new shoes hurt his feet, but Tony still played well.
4 For a year, Tony had lessons from Mr Gordon.
5 He married Linda when he was twenty.
6 He won the competition, and the next day his photograph was in the newspaper.
7 Mrs Wood bought him new clothes and shoes.
8 Now he is famous and has given thousands of concerts.
9 Then he went to the College of Music for three years.
10 One day Mr Gordon told him about a music competition in the town.

After Reading

1 This is the beginning of Sally Hill's story about Sir Anthony Evans. Can you find and correct the fourteen mistakes in it?

Yesterday was Sir Anthony Evans' seventieth birthday concert. He played music for the guitar by Mozart, and millions of people came to listen to this very famous guitarist. After the concert, I went to see him and his sister, Lady Linda Evans, in the theatre dressing-room, and Sir Anthony told me his story.

He came second in a music competition when he was sixteen, but the story really began before that. One day in an old factory building a boy called Tony found a new piano. He was fourteen at the time. He came from a musical family and he knew a lot about music, and when he touched the keys of the piano . . .

2 Put these words into two lists. Then think of a name for each list and write them in the boxes.

animal, chicken, college, concert, country, cow, field, grass, keys, lorry, note, piano, play, practise, song, sound, yard

3 Sally Hill also talked to Lady Linda Evans about Sir Anthony. Put their conversation into the correct order and write in the speakers' names. Sally speaks first (number 3).

1 _____ 'When he played the piano that first time, I knew that he was a real musician – much more than me. And I wanted to help him.'

2 _____ 'How did you feel when he won the competition?'

3 _____ 'What was Sir Anthony like when you first met him?'

4 _____ 'It was wonderful! I was so happy for him. He went away after that, of course – but he always came back.'

5 _____ 'Why did you want to teach him?'

6 _____ 'I didn't want to tell anybody. It was our secret. Tony liked learning about music – and I liked being with Tony.'

7 _____ 'He was a big, strong boy. He didn't say very much, but he was very nice.'

8 _____ 'Why didn't you tell your parents about the lessons?'

9 _____ 'Oh yes! He learnt very quickly, and he remembered everything.'

10 _____ 'So you taught him to read music. Was he a good student?'

4 Here is a new illustration for the story. Find the best place
in the story to put the picture, and answer these questions.

The picture goes on page _____.

1 Where are these people?
2 Who are they helping, and why?
3 What happened earlier that evening?

Now write a caption for the illustration.

Caption: _____

5 Write in the names which go best with these descriptions.

Mr and Mrs Wood / Mr Gordon / Mrs Lark / Linda Wood / Pip and John / Tony's mother

1 _____ helped Tony to move the piano.
2 _____ gave Tony time for his piano lessons, and paid for his lessons at the College of Music.
3 _____ gave Tony his first piano lessons free.
4 _____ got a job for him on Mr Wood's farm.
5 _____ taught Tony to read music.
6 _____ taught Tony to enjoy singing.

Whose help do you think was most important to Tony? Put the names of the characters in order, with the most important one first.

6 Do you agree (A) or disagree (D) with these sentences? Explain why.

1 If you have a special feeling for music (or football, or writing), you don't have to work hard or practise every day.
2 If you want to be really good at something, it must be the most important thing in your life.
3 Luck is more important than hard work if you want to do well.
4 If you want to do well, the most important thing is to belong to a rich family.

ABOUT THE AUTHOR

Rosemary Border is a very experienced teacher and writer, who has also worked as an editor, a lawyer, and a journalist. She is the author of a great number of books for learners of English – more than she can remember. 'I stopped counting after 150,' she says. She has written or retold more than 80 graded readers, including several stories for the Oxford Bookworms Library. Among these are *The Lottery Winner* (an original story, at Stage 1) and *Tooth and Claw* (a collection of short stories by Saki, at Stage 3). She lives and works in Suffolk, in the east of England.

ABOUT BOOKWORMS

OXFORD BOOKWORMS LIBRARY

Classics • True Stories • Fantasy & Horror • Human Interest
Crime & Mystery • Thriller & Adventure

The OXFORD BOOKWORMS LIBRARY offers a wide range of original and adapted stories, both classic and modern, which take learners from elementary to advanced level through six carefully graded language stages:

Stage 1 (400 headwords)	**Stage 4** (1400 headwords)
Stage 2 (700 headwords)	**Stage 5** (1800 headwords)
Stage 3 (1000 headwords)	**Stage 6** (2500 headwords)

More than fifty titles are also available on cassette, and there are many titles at Stages 1 to 4 which are specially recommended for younger learners. In addition to the introductions and activities in each Bookworm, resource material includes photocopiable test worksheets and Teacher's Handbooks, which contain advice on running a class library and using cassettes, and the answers for the activities in the books.

Several other series are linked to the OXFORD BOOKWORMS LIBRARY. They range from highly illustrated readers for young learners, to playscripts, non-fiction readers, and unsimplified texts for advanced learners.

Oxford Bookworms Starters	*Oxford Bookworms Factfiles*
Oxford Bookworms Playscripts	*Oxford Bookworms Collection*

Details of these series and a full list of all titles in the OXFORD BOOKWORMS LIBRARY can be found in the *Oxford English* catalogues. A selection of titles from the OXFORD BOOKWORMS LIBRARY can be found on the next pages.

Matty Doolin

CATHERINE COOKSON

Retold by Diane Mowat

Matty is fifteen and is leaving school in a few weeks' time. He wants to work with animals, and would like to get a job on a farm. But his parents say he's too young to leave home – he must stay in the town and get a job in ship-building, like his father. They also say he can't go on a camping holiday with his friends. And they say he can't keep his dog, Nelson, because Nelson barks all day and eats his father's shoes.

But it is because of Nelson that Matty finds a new life . . .

Too Old to Rock and Roll and Other Stories

JAN MARK

Retold by Diane Mowat

Greg is a teenager with a problem – his father. After the death of Greg's mother in an accident, his father takes no interest in life at all. Greg tries hard to help him. His father is too old to rock and roll, of course . . . or is he?

These short stories by Jan Mark look at life, love, and friendship through teenagers' eyes.

BOOKWORMS • TRUE STORIES • STAGE 2

The Love of a King

PETER DAINTY

All he wanted to do was to marry the woman he loved. But his country said 'No!'

He was Edward VIII, King of Great Britain, King of India, King of Australia, and King of thirty-nine other countries. And he loved the wrong woman.

She was beautiful and she loved him – but she was already married to another man.

It was a love story that shook the world. The King had to choose: to be King, or to have love . . . and leave his country, never to return.

BOOKWORMS • TRUE STORIES • STAGE 2

William Shakespeare

JENNIFER BASSETT

William Shakespeare. Born April 1564, at Stratford-upon-Avon. Died April 1616. Married Anne Hathaway: two daughters, one son. Actor, poet, famous playwright. Wrote nearly forty plays.

But what was he like as a man? What did he think about when he rode into London for the first time . . . or when he was writing his plays *Hamlet* and *Romeo and Juliet* . . . or when his only son died?

We know the facts of his life, but we can only guess at his hopes, his fears, his dreams.

BOOKWORMS • HUMAN INTEREST • STAGE 2

Stories from the Five Towns

ARNOLD BENNETT

Retold by Nick Bullard

Arnold Bennett is famous for his stories about the Five Towns and the people who live there. They look and sound just like other people, and, like all of us, sometimes they do some very strange things. There's Sir Jee, who is a rich businessman. So why is he making a plan with a burglar? Then there is Toby Hall. Why does he decide to visit Number 11 Child Row, and who does he find there? And then there are the Hessian brothers and Annie Emery – and the little problem of twelve thousand pounds.

BOOKWORMS • HUMAN INTEREST • STAGE 3

'Who, Sir? Me, Sir?'

K. M. PEYTON

Retold by Diane Mowat

Sam Sylvester is a teacher who wants his class to have ambition, and to do great things in life. So he enters them for a sporting competition against the rich students of Greycoats School.

The team that he has chosen for the competition think Sam has gone crazy. 'Who, Sir? Me, Sir?' says little Hoomey, his eyes round with horror. 'We'll never beat Greycoats,' the others cry. 'Never in a million years!'

But you don't know what you can do – until you try . . .